LIVING, *Loving* AND LOATHING

• • • • • • • • • •

**MODERN RHYMES AND LIMERICKS
FOR THE ROMANTICALLY INCLINED
AND HUMOROUSLY CORRECT**

MICHAEL CRAIG DANIELS

GOOD KNIGHT BOOKS

Living, Loving and Loathing
Published by
Good Knight Books
P.O. Box 373
Bailey, Colorado 80421-0373

Copyright © 1998 by Michael Craig Daniels
All rights reserved. No portion of this book may be reproduced—mechanically, electronically, or by any other means, including photocopying—without the written permission of the publisher, except brief inclusions of quotations in connection with a review in a magazine or newspaper.

Jacket and book design by Karen Groves
Illustrations Copyright © 1997 Karen Groves
The following trademarks appear throughout the book:
Oreo® and Nestlé® Quik®
Library of Congress Catalog Card Number: 97-94240
First Edition
ISBN 0-9659946-2-7
Printed in the United States of America by BookCrafters on acid-free, elementally chlorine-free paper.

To Merlyn

We shared your lifetime together.
I watched you grow,
And I loved you so.
You were my best friend.
A loyal and true friend.
And you'll always be
A part of me. . .
Forever.

I followed rivers
Flowing with dreams,
You were behind,
Following me.
I was your hero.
I was your life.
I hope that you knew,
You were mine too.

Wherever I'd be,
You'd be with me.
You guided my ways
Through happy days
And this is for you!

Contents

To Merlyn iii
Caveat vii

LIVING

At Twenty One 3
The Harvest House 5
How to Woo a Woman 7
No Time for Me 11
Eggcetera 13
The Climber 15
Her Name is Sarah 17
Another Misnomer 19
Happy 21 21
Friends 23
It Could Happen to You 25
Military Blues 27
An RSVP from Me 29
Ours to Win 31

Loving

To Live and Love 35
I've Never Really Loved 37
On Love 39
Sure Would be Easy 41
Unrequited Love 43

SO FAR AWAY	45
CARA BONITA	47
A DREAM COME TRUE	49
DON'T SAY NO	51
TO THE SKY	53
DAYS BEHIND	55
THROUGH IRISH EYES	57
COLLEEN	59
UPS AND DOWNS	61
"IN LOVE" ... AGAIN!	63

LOATHING

MY TURN	67
TIRED AND SORRY	69
IT COULD HAVE BEEN ME	71
SO SHE'S MARRIED	73
GOODBYE	75
I MUST RETORT	77
BEAUTY SANS GRACE	79
ANOTHER YEAR	81
EXCUSE ME FOR LIVING	83
I WANT A STATUE	85

CAVEAT

The following lines
Are nothing but rhymes,
Poems the way they should be!

These are my views
Which I hope will amuse
Or regale to some small degree.

With each page you turn
You're likely to learn
Something you may want to use.

Quoting's okay,
As long as you pay
This rightful author his due!

Please go ahead
Now that you've read
The words appearing above,

I think you're prepared
For the verse that I've shared
On Living, Loathing and Love.

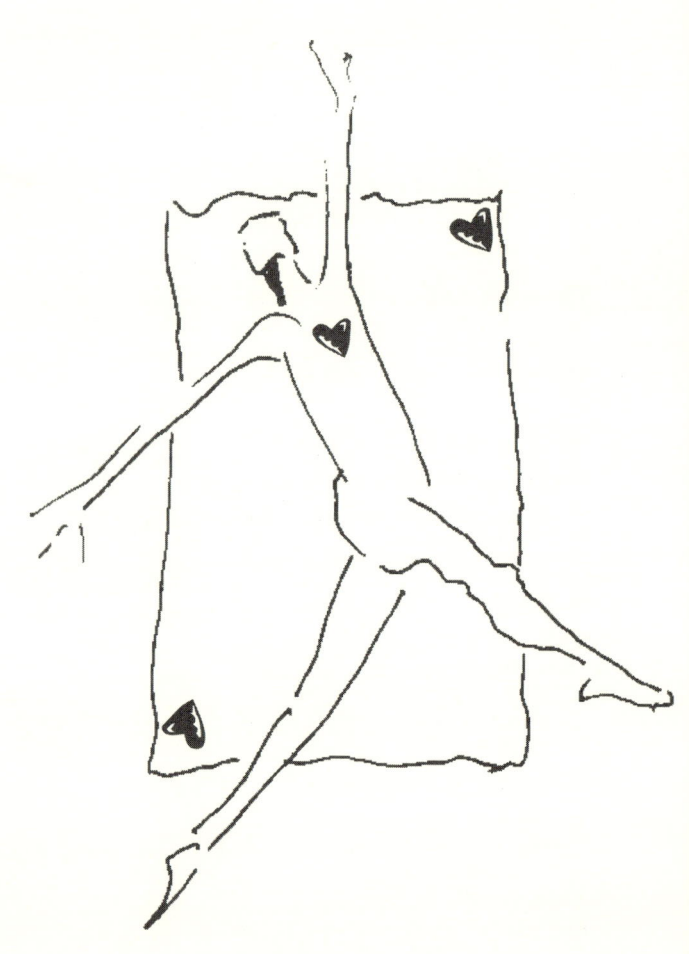

LIVING

At Twenty One

I met her playin' Twenty-One,
No lady luck,
Nowhere to run.
And when my chips were gettin' low
She dealt these words you see below:

Life is full of gambles,
All's fair in love and war.
And if there is no risk involved,
It's not worth playin' for.

We bluff through most our lives,
While rarely cashin' in,
So when the cards are dealt our way,
It's time to play to win.

With faces down no one knows,
They're forced to try and guess.
To fold is to surrender
To those who might hold less.

So ante up and play your hand,
Cut the cards and deal 'em.
Do the best with what you're dealt—
In Latin: Carpe Diem!

THE HARVEST HOUSE

There's a funny kind of feelin'
Seems I've been here once before,
I see familiar faces
As I step in through the door.
The people comin' toward me
And the voices that I hear,
Remind me of another time
Or place or so I fear.
My heartbeat starts to quicken,
Could this be some déja vu?
Naw, it's just coincidence,
There's nothin' wrong with you.
So I look at all the women
Just lookin' at my face,
All those painted ladies
Dressed to hide their lack of grace!
Hit the bar, see the tender,
Buy a beer and walk away,
Stand around and sip the suds
Just to rate the "fine" display.

Hurtin' dudes are all I see,
Lost in love and lost in life,
And hell there ain't no woman here
I'd take to be my wife!
All the time I see the same,
And still to me it's just a game.
Bars and pubs and discothéques
Respond to those who look for sex!
There are the kind who look for more
Than some coke or beer or cosmic whore!
So I guess I'll leave this Harvest House place
And head on home to my own space.
I'm trading in my swizzle stick
For Oreos® and Nestlé's® Quik®!
And to this scene I bid adieu,
And to all this wasted time,
Seems to me there's more to life
Than asking: *"What's your sign?"*

How To Woo A Woman

Women are smart,
Pretty and fun,
And life is too short
To settle on one.
So if there's a lass
Who catches your eye,
Follow these tips
I'm about to supply:

A nice place to dine
And a bottle of wine's
The standard from coast to coast,
But fresh chocolate cake
Or a tall chocolate shake
Will do the trick for most!

Depending on style
It's worth your while
To buy her a Teddy bear too.
I know it sounds dumb
But it works for some
And I offer it now to you.

And if you're like me
And like what you see,
You'll find her something to wear,
A woman looks best
When she's well dressed
So buy her some clothes *and* the bear!

When buying cologne
Don't buy her her own,
Have her try your favorite scent.
It's a known fact to me
That your olfactory
Works best when money's well spent!

Music and theater's
The best way to treat her
So plan on some tickets for shows.
And I'm sure you'll agree
No matter the fee,
The evening must start with a rose.

An invitation
For a weekend vacation
Is always a clever idea,
But if she says no
I want you to know
There's nothing at all to fear.

For some women dread
Sharing a bed
And that's an understandable thing.
Romancing's okay
But they'll hit the hay
Only when wearing a ring!

A cold winter's night
By warm firelight
Will soon find her in your arms.
Then what you do
Is all up to you
And your own personal charms!

When all's said and done
And you've chosen just one
No other you woo could replace.
You need not woo more
She's what you wooed for
And wooing is just for the chase!

No Time For Me

Arriving at work
She beats the clock
Puts on her fake smile.
And so to sell clothes
She says her hellos
But thinks of her life all the while.
All of her time
Just wasting away
Learning 'bout earning her keep,
Day after day
No time to play
Maybe four hours of sleep.
Walking around
Beating her brain:
"Why am I even here?"
Tells all the world
It's only for now
Just waiting for one more year.
The pay's below par
And spent on her car
Nothing to set herself free.

So she goes on
Just holding on
And not where she wants to be!
She has to do this
She has to do that
She has to get ready for work,
When she's at home
She's never alone
Thanks to her brother, the jerk!
Takes no advice
And so pays the price
Of being too blind to see,
Her life is before her
And I just adore her
But she has no time for me!

EGGCETERA

Toss me that egg,
    I said, I said.
Toss me that egg, I said.
    I don't want it scrambled,
    I don't want it poached,
    Sunny-side up or on top of my toast,
Just toss me that egg, I said!

Don't crack my egg,
    I beg, I beg.
Don't crack my egg, I beg.
    Hard boiled's okay
    But please not today,
Just toss me that egg, I said.
    I don't want it fried,
    No omelet with cheese,

Just toss me that egg,
      I beg of you please!
      The chicken that laid it
      Is somehow related
      to brother or sister or me.
      That egg is a cousin,
      Just one of a dozen,
      And not what it's cracked up to be!

So handle with care
      The egg you have there,
Just toss it on over I plead.
      That little round yolk
      Is little kin folk,
      Much more than an egg, indeed!

THE CLIMBER

Timberline
As far as the eye can see.
Night draws upon him
And he's not where he wants to be.
The summit is up there,
Piercing the thin air,
And though he's behind,
He's bound to climb
His mountain.

Where others have failed
He has prevailed.
There's no looking down
So far from the ground
On his mountain.
The climber he knows
The snow comes and goes
As he works his way.
To climb up the rocks
He dodges the knocks
So his ropes don't fray.
He slips and he falls,
Stumbles and crawls,
But will not delay
The climb up his mountain.

The clouds that surround him
Like pillows around him
Soften the climb still ahead.
He won't stop to rest
In search of his quest
And so he climbs on instead.

Tired and weak
Nearing the peak
It's hand over hand
Until he can stand
On his mountain.

The pinnacle his,
The top of the biz,
Worth all the bruises and bumps?
But with nowhere to climb
He loses his mind
And runs to the edge and jumps!

Her Name Is Sarah

Listen to the tale I tell:
Her name is Sarah, not Michelle!
And so it goes
I sent a rose
Along with quotation.
Then I chose
A second rose
To add to my flirtation.
I never knew
Just who was who
I asked a friend you see.
I described
And he supplied
The name he thought was she.
The words were sent
With good intent,
Romantic and refined.
I left no clue, She never knew,
My name was never signed.
And so to close
There is no rose
For you the unintended.
Were this in jest
I could not best
This tale I've just now ended!

"What's in a name?

That which we call a rose

by any other name would

smell as sweet!"
—William Shakespeare

ANOTHER MISNOMER

Were I not me
And she not she
I wouldn't even bother,
But I *am* he who foolishly
Mistook her for another.
So now I must
Regain her trust
In somewhat of a twit,
There's not much time
To wine and dine,
I must rely on wit!
I'll find a way
With words to say
How much I'd like to know her.
I'm more than a gent,
I'm intel-li-gent,
And *that* I plan to show her.
Unlike her beaus
I'll send a rose
With words composed in rhyme.
With no misnomer
I'll hand it over
And hope she's she this time!

HAPPY 21

Happy Twenty-One
Your legal life's begun.
At this age they say
To do as you may
But when it's okay, it's not fun!

This age is best
Which turns the page
And chapter one appears,
May yours read well
Of love and life
And so throughout your years.

That time is best
Which opens minds
And hearts are set at ease,
May time be yours
To live, to learn,
To fill your memories.

FRIENDS

Friends are our strength
In body and soul,
They stand by our side
When years take their toll.
They're there to confide in,
They're there for the ride,
They count on each other,
No promise denied.

Friends give us courage
To fight the good fight.
They help without asking
When others take flight.
They're there when there's sorrow,
They're there when we cry,
True friends are a gift
No money can buy!

And so as your age
Continues to climb
Rejoice in the friends
You've gathered through time.

It Could Happen To You

His arms were longing for a love to hold.
His heart was waiting for a tale untold.
Her breath would warm him
   till the morning sun.
He didn't love her, it was just for fun!
He never would have loved her so,
If he were sober he'd have let her go.
She held him captive with endearing eyes
As he held her with enchanting lies.
The night brought him to her arms,
The night lost him to her charms.
He didn't want to say he loved her.
He only wanted to make love to her.
On lust and greed his instincts ran
And in just one night new life began!
Lucky for him just life was emitted,
It could have been worse
Had disease been transmitted!
"A condom a date keeps the baby away"
So best be prepared if you're straight or gay!
And if you're like this poor young lover,
Take some advice and wear a rubber!

MILITARY BLUES

Marching is an art
That I could live without.
Inspection is okay
Until I'm singled out!

I've learned our nation's secrets
Perhaps a bit too well,
I'd like to share them with you
But I'm not allowed to tell!

I shine my shoes, I make my bed,
I even wear a tie,
And if I do those well enough
They may just let me fly!

I won't complain, I will not whine,
I'll do all things their way,
Our sergeant sings us show tunes
And no one thinks he's gay!

With all this spit and polish
I think I'm going blind,
In four more years of service
I may just lose my mind!

An R.S.V.P. From Me

Like a Spielberg production
With no introduction
I shook the hands of time.
I didn't know then
And still don't know now,
It happened so fast
I can't explain how.

It just took a moment,
A blink of an eye,
But all that I asked
Was met with reply.
Where are we going
And where have we been?
Was there an Eden
And did Eve sin?

Should I attend
A Christmas affair?
Will all of my favorite
Cookies be there?

He had an answer
Whatever the query,
But as for the party
He was a bit leery!

"It's doubtful a party
Your company throws
Will offer you milk
And fresh Oreos.®
But no matter the fare
It's best that you show,
You might get a raise
For braving the snow!"

"Bring your old dog,
Your very best friend,
An excuse to leave early
Sometime before ten."
So on his advice
We R.S.V.P.,
And I'll keep the dog
Away from the tree!

Ours To Win

Not all times are best of times,
Not all moments great.
We reap the seeds we sow
Or leave it up to fate.

Amid the love and laughter
There's pain and sorrow too,
And when we feel the latter,
The former gets us through.

Who can say what lies ahead?
Who knows what's not yet been?
The past is lost forever,
The future's ours to win!

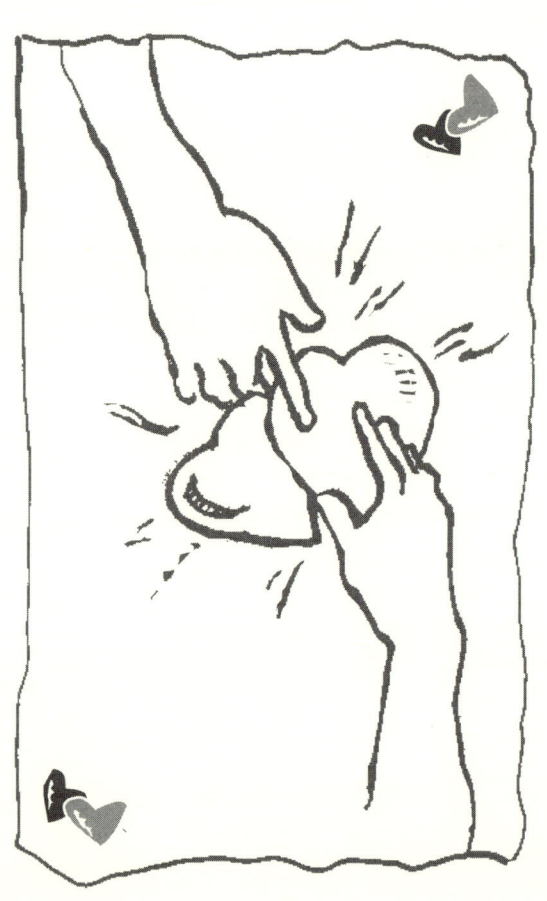

Loving
. . . .

To Live and Love

It's easy to live and love
And many have done just so,
But living and loving exacts a price
And that you'll come to know.

Many misunderstand it,
And many just don't care,
But if you've yet to live and love
I bid you all beware!

Love is such a tender word
Though often used in vain,
For just as you have loved and lost
You're sure to love again!

Living is what you do.
Loving is from within.
And both are full of hopes and dreams
And all that might have been.

No warning will suffice.
No tales of woe will do.
Love claims so many broken hearts
You'll be a victim too!

I'VE NEVER REALLY LOVED

Through the years
and days gone by,
I've often thought
and wondered why...
I've never really loved.

When I think of all
the girls I've known,
The past affairs,
the wild oats sown,
The chances lost,
the lessons learned,
The games I've played
where tables turned. . .
I've never really loved.

And perhaps I never will. . .
But even if I do,
I know I'll never find
another one like you!

On Love

Some love too little
Some too well,
Some just love,
To kiss and tell.
Some love the voice,
Some the eyes,
Some a dream
In human guise.
Some love the words,
Some the deeds.
Some the fire
Which love feeds.
Perhaps it's lust that casts the spark.
Or maybe Cupid hits his mark.
Then, in the heat of passion's lure,
Love is forged forevermore.
The mind desires,
The heart demands,
The soul responds
But love commands.
And if you find these words untrue,
Then love has yet to meet with you!

Sure Would Be Easy

It sure would be easy
To write a few lines
Of sweet loving words
In rhythmical rhymes
For a gal who has warmed
The world I found cold
And makes my tomorrows
A dream to unfold.
But knowing the girl
As well as I do
I'm sure she would say:
"Did you really have to?"
Which leaves me to ponder
The methods at hand
To show this young lady
Just where I stand.
For try as I may
To foster some trust
She still won't believe
It's more than just lust!
I so want to hold her
And lay by her side,
I so want to tell her
All that I've tried.

But whatever I do
And whatever I say,
Must meet with approval
Before it's okay!
It sure would be easy
To have someone who
Allowed me to love them
As I love you!

UNREQUITED LOVE

Why don't you see me like I see you?
Why don't you feel like I feel for you?
Is the reason unfair?
Is it just you don't care for me?
Am I living in a dream
And not reality?

Why are you so beautiful to me?
Why is time so wonderful
   when you're with me?
Is it just I don't know
How to touch you?
Is it just I'm not the type
You're attracted to?

Why don't you see me as others do?
Where is the warmth I only wish I knew?
If it's just another love
I wouldn't give a damn,
But I think that it's because
Of who I am.

What can I do to make amends with you?
Will I ever be more than
   just a friend to you?
Is there someone from your past
I remind you of
That you took a chance on once
And fell in love?
Why must you play the games that you do?
Why don't you love me as I love you?

So Far Away

So far away and still I see
A loving smile meant for me,
That lights my days and lingers on
While others' meet oblivion.

An empty hand and yet I know
The warmth and touch that I love so,
Of soft caress and sweet embrace
That photographs cannot replace.

No words are said but still I hear
The tender voice that calms my fear,
And shelters me till morning's kiss
Of which I'll add I also miss!

These thoughts of you will have to do,
They're all I have to see me through
The lonely nights without you.

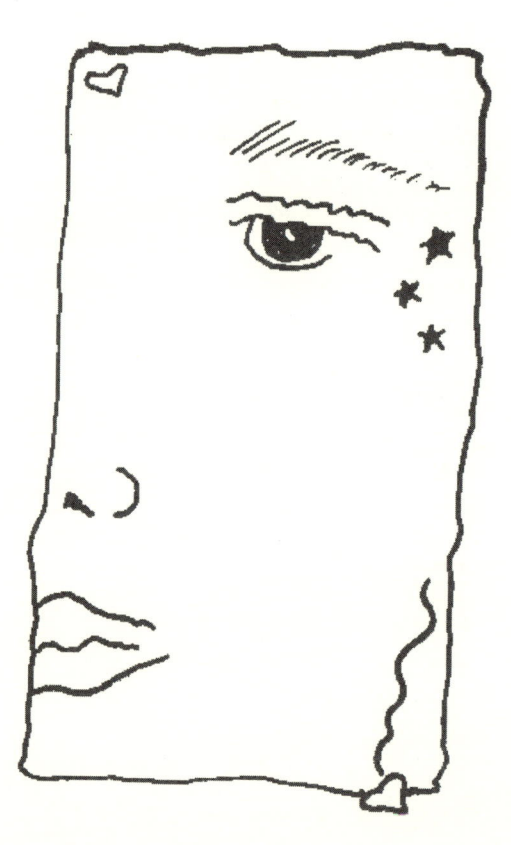

Cara Bonita

There's a dream many have
Seems that I have it too,
Of the perfect girl
Who's been waiting for you.
Though reality shames us
And the dream slips away,
I still keep believing
That I'll find her someday.
I know in my heart
That she has to exist,
For though I've held others,
T'was her that I kissed!
There are beauties I meet
Even I could adore,
And at times I wonder
What I'm looking for,
But I know she's out there
Waiting for me somewhere.
Cara Bonita I love you.
There's nothing they say,
There's nothing they do
That will ever stop me
From looking for you.
Oh Cara Bonita where are you?

A Dream Come True

There's a dream many have,
Guess that I've had it too,
Of a girl you've always known
But whose face you never knew.

And when your eyes are closed
You know where she will be,
There within your dream
She waits so patiently.

Her name you can't recall,
Her voice is not quite clear,
And when she fades away
You know she'll reappear.

But now at last I think I know
Who in this dream I love,
For when I close my eyes
It's you I'm dreaming of!

Don't Say No

Don't say no.
    I just want some attention.
Don't say good night.
    You don't know my intention.

Don't think what you're thinking,
    I want more than that.
Don't flatter yourself
    You're already flat!

You don't give out and that's okay,
    You're more than just one night,
You're such a pretty lady
    And deserve your Mister Right.

But it could be that I am he
    Just waiting at your door,
So take a chance on this romance
    With hopes it's so much more.

Let me go, you'll never know
    If what I say is true,
And so I beg with bended leg
    For just one night with you!

To The Sky

Flying around careless and free
I had no ropes to hold on to me.
Soaring so high, dancing on air,
I looked below and found you there.

I need the bright warm rays of the sun
If I am to do the things I've yet done.
My feathers are ruffled,
   my stay nears its end,
It's happened before, it'll happen again.
Here in the clouds I'm in command
Of all of the hopes and dreams
   that I've planned.
The sky is the freedom I need to explore,
Take hold of my hand but please, nothing
   more!

I should have never opened my wings
If love is the ending the fairy tale brings.
Touching the ground is all part of living,
I'm good at the touching
   but not at the giving!
I'll fly to the north as you fly west
And we'll let the seasons be love's nest.

If we return and find it warm,
Then we can say our love is born.
The sky is the freedom we need to explore,
And love is a mountain
    we need not look for,
But if all we can find are the hills
    and the glens,
Then we'll have to settle
    on just being friends.

DAYS BEHIND

Though we've drawn apart
And left our days behind,
I'd like to say my thoughts;
That is if you don't mind.

Many times I tried to say
Just how much I loved you.
Many times the words failed
And so you never knew.

Now when words mean little,
I find it hard to say these few,
But now there is no better time
For me to say I loved you!

I realize I was wrong
And cannot make amends,
But I hope that once lovers
You and I can still be friends.

THROUGH IRISH EYES

I spied a bonny lass within me view
With bonny eyes so big and blue.
Of those that's here I fancy one
Were not fer her I'd fancy none.

Just who is she this maiden fair
Who, after work, lets down her hair?
There's somethin' 'bout her that's fer sure,
And what it is must be her lure!

What kind of woman might she be?
And is there more I've yet to see?
The answers would no doubt unfold
This bonny lass me eyes behold.

Me sole intent is purely good
But we'll ne'er meet fer ne'er we should.
'Tis fer the best, me bonny one
As nothin' ends which ne'er begun!

I think no harm in verse there be,
What finer form of flattery?
And so fer thee composed these lines
In proper time fer Valentine's!

COLLEEN

You . . . Pretty Colleen,
You . . . With your hair of gold,
You . . . With your eyes of green
That share an emerald's hue!

You . . . Look at me and smile
And bliss is mine for a while.
You're a gem that shines
And you'll age like wine
As you grow from a princess to a queen.
Like a diamond cut fine
By the hands of time
You're beautiful, Colleen!

Ups And Downs

We deserve a better time,
A chance to make it through.
With all the ups and downs,
I still keep loving you.

At times I see no end
To what's been in our way,
Yet I keep holding on
When I should walk away.

We'll share the highs and lows,
My friend, my love, my guide.
No matter where life leads
I'll be there by your side!

"In Love"... Again!

Every now and then I love,
Or so I think I do.
I don't know why it is,
But I'm in love with you!

All is fair in love they say
So I have stacked the cards,
Though through the years
Some hands I've dealt
Were full of broken hearts.
I've had my share of winning hands,
I've lost a few as well,
But this is one I will not lose
As time alone will tell.

This is more than all of those
Where love had no real part,
I never truly loved before
But I'm prepared to start!

LOATHING

. . . .

My Turn

How could you leave me?
I thought you cared.
Not once were your feelings
Openly aired!

You just left me a note
With the hate that you wrote
And walked out without a good by.
You took what was mine,
Including my time,
And I think I deserve to know why!

You know me too well
To think it ends here.
I've got something to say
That you're gonna hear:

I really don't care
That you walked out on me,
My only concern
Is you have my TV!

And with all that you took
It's a comfort to know
That although you tried,
My dog wouldn't go!

I thought I'd be kind
And let bygones be,
But then I decided
That just isn't me!

Someday you'll learn
That I've tied the knot,
And whoever she'll be
Is someone you're not!

You, bounced all your checks,
Denied me good sex,
And made my life a mess.
I lived with your ways
And cursed all the days
You suffered from PMS!

It's easy to hate
When bidding farewell,
So I'll wish you the best
ON YOUR WAY TO HELL!

TIRED AND SORRY

I've written all the words I can write for you,
I've said all the things I can say,
I try to reason why it is
You make me feel this way.
You say you have some trials,
You say you have no time,
I've given all I can for you
To try to make you mine,

But I'm tired.
I'm tired of being alone.
I've waited far too long for you
And still I'm on my own.
Others might have walked away
Just giving up on you,
But I'm the type who takes the chance
And bears to see it through.

The world will keep on turnin'
And time will pass along,
I know I have my life to live
And blaming you is wrong,
But I'm tired.

I'm tired of waiting for you.
All I have are fading dreams
And wishes to come true.
You say I have no right or cause
To feel the way I do
And lately when I close my eyes
I loathe the thought of you!

I know that when I say good-bye,
There'll be no second chance,
I'm moving on to better times,
And to someone who can dance!
You think you've got it all,
Good looks and not a care,
But in the end you'll find yourself
Upon your derrière!

I'm sorry.
I'm sorry 'bout things I might say.
I only want to be with you
And haven't found a way,
So I'm sorry!
I'm sorry I showed how I cared.
I tried to give you everything
And this is how I fared.

It Could Have Been Me

It could have been me
In tails by her side,
It could have been me
In love with this bride.
It could have,
It should have,
It might have been.
Whatever the reasons,
She's now with him!
You had her,
He has her,
It's all said and done.
He'll love her for life,
You loved her for fun!
Admit it,
You blew it,
You had your chance.
So swallow your pride
And ask her to dance.
Wish her the best
And just walk away.
Think of her friends
As possible prey!

So She's Married

Although you wear a ring
And share a home for two,
I see no reason why
I can't go out with you!
Dating would be tough,
You don't want an affair.
I know you have a guy right now
But how about a spare?
Call me when you can
See me when you're able,
Think of it this way. . .
You've added to your stable!
I know you've tied the knot
For that is plain to see,
You may be married now
But not so happily!
So if you change your name
And find you're on your own,
Share the news with me
And make your "status" known.
At which time if you prefer
I'll be there by your side,
Or if so inclined
I'll take you as *my* bride!

GOOD BYE

And so to good bye,
A word withheld till the end.
I've said it before
And many times more
I'll say it again!

And so we must part,
As others have done through time.
There's no grand adieu
For me and you,
Just your farewell and mine.

I Must Retort

You question words I say
And I needn't tell you why,
But you have to have an answer
So I make up some reply.
I always find the words
And try to be polite,
I say what's on my mind
Be it wrong or be it right!
Tact is just another word
For lying through your teeth,
And I claim to be above
Because I know I'm not beneath!
I make the point well known
That I'm my own best friend,
And when confined with lesser sorts
I'm forced to condescend!

Please don't get me wrong,
I won't be second guessed.
There are those I'm civil to
Though few I must confess.
I now appeal to all of you,
My manner quite sublime—
You'll never know a better man,
Mortal or divine!
To think of me a snob
Would truly be unfair,
Yet I admit I've given cause
To point a "finger" there!
It's true my way offends
But that's just how I am.
Regardless of your thoughts,
I just don't give a damn!
So leave me to myself.
It's best that you take heed.
For I can be a bastard
Whenever there's the need!

BEAUTY SANS GRACE

I once wooed this lady
Who drove a Mercedes
And turned all men's heads driving by.

She's very well known,
Blue-blood to the bone,
And boasts what she owns and can buy.

She's a tease and a flirt
Who lifts up her skirt
Or unbuttons her shirt for display.

Don't try to undress her
Unless you impress her
With all the best toys of the day!

She's an upper class whore
With whom you can score
For a few dollars more than it's worth.

She's beauty sans grace,
She's vulgar and base
And there's no greater waste on this earth.

Perhaps you know of her
Perhaps you have loved her
Or have someone like her in mind.

But if you should date her
Use this to berate her
And maybe she'll turn out just fine!

ANOTHER YEAR

Your youth didn't last,
The future's now past
And time keeps on speeding ahead.

The girls you once harried
Are all grown and married
And most of your teachers are dead!

Though your vision has faded,
Your sanity's debated
And your bubble and fizz have gone flat,

You need not despair
For your health is still fair,
What more could a man want than that?

Another year's gone
And still you live on
While others are passing away.

Indeed you've outlasted
So many, you bastard,
And your hair has yet to turn gray!

EXCUSE ME FOR LIVING

I can say this on my behalf:
I say things that make one laugh,
And I've been wrong and I've been rude,
I'm an unabashed, self-righteous dude!
I reach for the stars and I reach for fame,
I want EVERYONE to know my name.
I adorn myself with fine attire,
And women are mine at my desire!
I plan my life from day to day,
And play life's game my own way.
I do what I want and always succeed
Without liquor, drugs or smoking weed!
I act like a gent with an air of Flynn,
And as an athlete, I like to win!
Yes, self-confidence can't be beat,
And believe me when I say it's not conceit.
I don't know why I am as I am,
And to be honest my friends,
I don't give a damn!
So excuse me for living,
I'm not sorry for my way.
Seems to me the world is mine
And I own every day.
Just excuse me for living!

I Want a Statue

There are some things in life
That money can't buy
No matter your wealth
Or how hard you try.
Hospital wings
Just bear a name
But statues are built
To those who earn fame.
Fame and glory
Cannot be bought.
They're only achieved
Through battles well fought.
Though some are content
With humble rewards
Like Mother Teresa
Who cared for the hordes,
I want a statue
Of bronze, gold or stone
So I'll live my days
To make my name known.

Wherever erected
And however tall,
I just want my statue known to all!
A fine sculpted form
Uniquely rare,
With a warning to pigeons:
"Don't even dare!"